WORK
EXCELLENCE

A Biblical Perspective *of* Work

CHARLES M. GARRIOTT

WORK

EXCELLENCE

A Biblical Perspective *of* Work

CHARLES M. GARRIOTT

RIOTT

Washington D.C.

Interior design by Jeffrey M. Hall, ION Graphic Design Works

Printed in the United States of America

Library of Congress Control Number: 2004098270

ISBN 0-9762004-0-6

1 2 3 4 5 6 7 8 9 10 / 10 09 08 07 06 05

www.workexcellence.net

To Debby, my wife

ACKNOWLEDGMENTS

I would not have written on the topic of work had it not been for the encouragement of my friends in Manila, Niels and Amyjay Riconalla.

Barbara Harley spent countless hours scrubbing this work and coaching me through it. The same is true for Maria Garriott, my sister-in-law. I am very much indebted to them. Many who live in other parts of the world gave me their insights as to the usefulness of the material as they read it. My time invested pales in comparison to the sum of my friends' efforts. Thank you all for your prayers and acts of love.

CONTENTS

PERSPECTIVE

I learned about work as a young boy. Growing up in a farming community outside Baltimore, I saw my father and grandfather hard at work in their respective trades. Grandfather Lehmann was a carpenter during the day and a farmer when he returned home. Soon after finishing high school my father entered the plumbing trade. Within a few years he managed his own plumbing business. Both men built their own homes. Each knew what it meant to work long days. These men were colorful examples of the attractions and rewards of work. I found their display of physical strength and skill with tools intoxicating.

When I was nine, Grandfather Lehmann allowed me to take a turn plowing the field with his Massey Ferguson tractor. What a privilege, I thought, to engage in the activity of men! During adolescence my father let me work with one of his mechanical crews as a "gofer." What is a gofer? A gofer stood near one of the plumbers and when he needed a tool, a piece of pipe, or something else from the truck, he would "go for" it. What a boring job! As time went on I learned skills which made the work more interesting. Often it was very demanding and hard. Sometimes I spent days digging ditches to lay sewer pipe, or I crawled around suffocating attics in the midsummer heat. But in addition to being in the company of men who knew the meaning of work, I got paid! It was not very much at first, but it was real money!

By the age of 18 I had learned not only some basic skills but also a definite view of work. I never paused, at that time, to consider the perspective I had developed regarding my day's activities. However, a philosophy of work had emerged.

Many years have passed since those childhood days. Eventually I finished my education and entered the ministry. As a pastor I spent time with friends whose occupations represented careers and the variety of work that exists in business, medicine, education, government and law enforcement. Some were executives, others politicians, judges, secretaries, or administrative assistants. Some friends worked in the military, and others were carpenters or mechanics. They represented both "white" and "blue-collar" work. Many had taken positions or jobs based upon their desired careers. Others had taken particular positions because those had been the only jobs offered to them.

We all need some form of employment in order to support families and ourselves. Most of us do not have the option of doing whatever we want with our time. Work is a necessity.

Our lives, and even our self-images and identities, are directly impacted by our careers. If we lose a job and have difficulty finding a new one, we may experience some degree of hopelessness and depression. Few things have a greater impact upon life than our work.

Many Christians never have thought about work from a biblical perspective. Although our hearts belong to Christ, too often our minds are held captive by the world. Our experiences and education tend to come from a secular viewpoint, especially regarding work. What does it mean to have a biblical perspective of work and the workplace? Do you understand the "glory of God" in your work? Do you pridefully boast (to yourself or others) about what you have accomplished? Do you think that church and home are the places to be Christian, but that work is secular and separate from your faith?

What may be good work to the world may be nothing more than "filthy rags" in God's sight. If it's "all about me," and God's glory isn't seen in my work, I haven't met the biblical standard of excellence:

> *...in order that in everything God may be glorified through Jesus Christ. To him belong glory and dominion forever and ever. Amen.*
>
> (I PETER 4:11B ESV)

The standard for the Christian when it comes to work is set forth in I Peter 1:

but as he who called you is holy, you also be holy in
all your conduct.

(v. 15 ESV)

As you proceed in this book on excellence in work, I hope
you will see that the Christian standard of excellence calls us
to holiness and gives God alone all the glory for every good
thing He enables us to do in each and every area of our lives.

CHAPTER 1

NEED FOR EXAMINATION

GOD is master over work. His Word addresses the many complexities of our jobs and careers. The Bible provides analysis and directives on the topic of work. Often it speaks to the subject directly and, at other times, it assumes a foundation of truth from the reader. It may call us to reexamine our work, career views and practices. In the Matthew 25 parable, Jesus does just that:

> *Again, it will be like a man going on a journey, who called his servants and entrusted his property to them. To one he gave five talents of money, to another two talents, and to another one talent, each according to his ability. Then he went on his journey. The man who had received the five talents went at once and put his money to work and gained five more. So also, the one with the two talents gained*

two more. But the man who had received the one talent went off, dug a hole in the ground and hid his master's money. After a long time the master of those servants returned and settled accounts with them. The man who had received the five talents brought the other five. 'Master,' he said, 'you entrusted me with five talents. See, I have gained five more.' His master replied, 'Well done, good and faithful servant! You have been faithful with a few things; I will put you in charge of many things. Come and share your master's happiness!' The man with the two talents also came. 'Master,' he said, 'you entrusted me with two talents; see, I have gained two more.' His master replied, 'Well done, good and faithful servant! You have been faithful with a few things; I will put you in charge of many things. Come and share your master's happiness!' Then the man who had received the one talent came. 'Master,' he said, 'I knew that you are a hard man, harvesting where you have not sown and gathering where you have not scattered seed. So I was afraid and went out and hid your talent in the ground. See, here is what belongs to you.' His master replied 'You wicked, lazy servant! So you knew that I harvest where I have not sown and gather where I have not scattered seed? Well then, you should have put my money on deposit with the bankers, so that when I returned I would have received it back with interest. Take the talent from him and give it to the one who has the ten talents. For everyone who has will be given more, and he will have an abundance. Whoever does not have, even what he has will be taken from him. And throw that worthless servant outside, into the darkness, where there will be weeping and gnashing of teeth.'

(MATTHEW 25: 14-30)

In this parable, Christ calls His listeners to examine the use of their God-given talents and gifts in building the kingdom of God. The passage also provides important general insights into godly work and how we should view it.

The parable tells of three men who took on a very important position in an investment company. The three were each entrusted with assets to invest in whatever they thought wise and financially promising. They differed in experience and ability. Sometime later each would be required to stand for an audit and evaluation of the results.

Their 'boss' knew them well, and trusted them. He evidently had no desire to micromanage and watch their every move: these were investors with knowledge and experience. He had an awareness of their work and had evaluated their abilities. Because he thought that one could handle more assets than the others, he gave five times more to the one investor, and over twice as much to another.

The differences, as the story shows, were not only with abilities, but also with their views of work. According to the parable, the one-talent investor's immediate response reveals much about his understanding of work and about his own character. While his fellow investors managed their entrusted assets, he, too, was productive. In fact, as one who has worked as a laborer, I can identify with his activity. He took a tool for digging and created a hole, burying the assets that had been entrusted to him. He made a mental note of the place so that he could retrieve it at a later date. You might say in his defense that at least he had not stolen or lost it. What this third investor did the remaining time the owner was gone we do not know. What we do know is that he wasted his time and produced nothing of value. He had been given a job to complete, and he expended minimal effort.

In due time the lazy investor reaped the rewards of his decisions and use of time. When the owner returned, he required each of the investors to give an account of his activity. Consider the report given by the one-talent investor:

> Then the man who had received the one talent came. 'Master,' he said, 'I knew that you are a hard man, harvesting where you have not sown and gathering where you have not scattered seed. So I was afraid and went out and hid your talent in the ground. See, here is what belongs to you.'
>
> (MATTHEW 25:24-25)

This is indeed a sad picture that represents the way of many workers today. As is usually the case, his work showed his character. When his supervisor asked for a report of his work, he falsely charged the owner with unethical business practices to cover up his own poor job performance. It would have been easier for him to resign. The owner immediately saw what had taken place and accurately assessed the one-talent investor. He called him "wicked and lazy." The man was an evil liar who thought only of himself. He slandered the owner. The one-talent investor cared nothing for either the owner or his business. In fact, you could say that the one-talent investor was guilty of stealing. The asset should have produced some type of return instead of nothing. The owner had a good reason to be angry with the man. The failure to pursue excellence in work indicated that he had no appreciation of the significance and glory of work.

As our character works itself out in our day-to-day activities, it produces long-term results. He experienced the consequences of his misconduct and excuses. The little that this man had was taken from him, and he was thrown out into the darkness and its misery.

In contrast to this evil and lazy man, we have the other two investors. They had been quick to put the entrusted funds to work during the long absence of the owner. When it was time to give an account of their work, each had been able to demonstrate some success on his project.

Their work had paid off. They were productive. They gained a 100% return on their investment. In response, they heard the following words:

"Well done, good and faithful servant! You have been faithful with a few things; I will put you in charge of many things. Come and share your master's happiness!"

(MATTHEW 25:23)

Indeed, who would not want to hear such words? Perhaps we read the passage and respond, "I am like the first two investors: I am diligent in the use of my abilities and resources." Yet the passage should cause us all to question if, in fact, we are all right. Do we not need to examine our lives? Certainly the lazy investor did not think it important.

This parable teaches that the resources entrusted to us must be used properly as designed. This is true both for those who trust in Christ and experience His mercy and for those who do not. Everyone experiences God's presence in possessing resources and exercising the ability to put them to good use. The difference is that the believer acknowledges this, and the unbeliever does not.

What do we learn about a biblical view of work from this passage? We learn that work is not evil. We also see that to be self-absorbed or lazy is a form of stealing and dishonors God. Our abilities and resources belong to God, and we should honor Him in our work. It is our responsibility and privilege to develop our God-given resources, including time, talents and abilities.

When we understand work's significance and glory, we pursue it with excellence. In the workplace Christ will work in and through us. We may not always see the kind of return we would like, but to work as one who realizes that he or she is working for the King of kings will make a great difference. We need Christ to direct us in this area of life.

—— REFLECTION ——

What have you learned about the biblical view
of work and pursuing excellence in the
workplace from Matthew 25?

———

What is your attitude toward your present
circumstances at work?

———

What would happen if today your supervisor at work
evaluated your attitude and performance?

———

Who do you know that models excellence in
attitude and performance in work?

———

How does Christ impact this area of your life?

WORK EXCELLENCE

*L*ORD, show me Your evaluation of my attitude and performance when it comes to my work. By Your grace enable me to pursue work in a Christ-like manner. May my work reveal Your glory. Amen.

CHAPTER 2

THE GENESIS OF WORK

I N Genesis we read the conclusion of God's work of creation:

Thus the heavens and the earth were completed in all their vast array. By the seventh day God had finished the work he had been doing; so on the seventh day he rested from all his work.

(GENESIS 2: 1 -2)

Do you remember being asked as a child, "What do you want to do when you grow up"? As you came closer to finishing your schooling, did the pressure to know the answer to that haunting question increase? Perhaps you still wonder what you should be doing, or you may be one of many who wish they had made a different choice.

Although Genesis may not provide you with a specific answer to that sometimes-nagging question, what it does teach makes a big difference in how you use your time. The opening pages of the Bible have a lot to say about work; indeed, work provides the opening scene for God's revelation of Himself.

Because God has addressed the topic of work so prominently, it demands our consideration. After all, as the Author of work, He is the one who has defined it for all times. It is truly a holy area.

A HOLY MODEL

In the beginning God created the heavens and the earth. Now the earth was formless and empty, darkness was over the surface of the deep, and the Spirit of God was hovering over the waters. And God said, "Let there be light," and there was light. God saw that the light was good, and he separated the light from the darkness. God called the light "day," and the darkness he called "night." And there was evening, and there was morning—the first day.

(GENESIS I : I-5)

The activity of creation described here provides, among other things, the foundation for a biblical understanding of work. Reading through the first chapter, we see a pattern in this divine activity (vv.1-5). God's work was, by the power of His word, to establish from nothing every part of the universe.

At the end of each day He saw positive progress and development. That which He accomplished was characterized as "good" (v.4). Indeed, all that He made was pleasing to Him and was, therefore, declared "good." This assessment of each day's work defines the holy standard—goodness and perfection.

At each stage of creation, God identified or named that portion of the whole. In other words, after God created light by speaking it into existence, He gave it the name "day" and called the darkness "night." The concept of names comes from His creative process.

Next we see the end or completion of a period. The workday started, and then it ended, even though there was more to create. When God accomplished the work in its entirety, He recognized completion: nothing remained unfinished. God did all that He had purposed to do, and then He rested.

> *God saw all that he had made, and it was very good.*
> *And there was evening, and there was morning—*
> *the sixth day. Thus the heavens and the earth were*
> *completed in all their vast array. By the seventh day*
> *God had finished the work he had been doing; so on*
> *the seventh day he rested from all His work.*
>
> (GENESIS 1:31-2:2)

One other characteristic of the holy model that should be mentioned is that God very boldly placed His work on display. His work is still all very visible. Every day we marvel at His magnificent work of creation. The glory of His finished work causes us to better understand God Himself and His glory. As the Psalmist says, "The heavens declare the glory of God; the skies proclaim the work of his hands" (Psalm 19:1).

This is the height of excellence in work! History speaks about many talented people and great accomplishments. They are honored and recognized in many ways. And yet, no matter how great a human work, it pales terribly in comparison to the works of the God of the universe. God truly has defined excellence in work.

IN THE IMAGE OF GOD

The zenith of God's work took place on the sixth day, when He created Adam and Eve. Man was made distinctively different from all the rest of God's incredible creation, including the animals. Are there many similarities between man and animals? Yes. However, the important difference is revealed in Chapter 1, verse 26, when God declares, "Let us make man in our image, after our likeness...." To be made in the image of God means that we have characteristics and traits that belong to man alone and that exist in God and are from God. We have, for example, an incredible ability to reason, to be concerned with the past, present, and future. Detailed planning is a normal part of our thinking. Man has an enormous ability to create. First we conceive a picture of something in our minds. That picture drives us to bring it to reality. We see creative ability when a meal, in the making for several hours, finally is served.

Less than a mile from where I write in Washington, D.C., stands the National Cathedral. The first stone was laid in

1907, and the building was completed 87 years later. It is a magnificent structure of cut stone, built for the glory of God by men made in thc image of God. Even a child's hand-drawn picture of trees and sky, as simple as it may be, is a reminder of this truth. It should surprise no one that since God is a God of work, the desire to work is part of our nature. Our desire to be productive with time and resources signals that we are made in the image of God. The same desire reminds us that we are *divincly called* to engage in work. *The only thing secular about work is the way we view and treat it.*

The government of a nation has a deep interest in the employment of its citizens. Consider the mission statement for the United States Department of Labor:

> *The Department of Labor fosters and promotes the welfare of the job seekers, wage earners, and retirees of the United States by improving their working conditions, advancing their opportunities for profitable employment, protecting their retirement and health care benefits, helping employers find workers, strengthening free collective bargaining, and tracking changes in employment, prices, and other national economic measurements.*[1]

History informs us that people without work and the opportunity to find work can throw nations into conflict and war. The state's concern about employment through its Department of Labor is actually a ministry to the people of that

---

1. [http://www.dol.gov Mission Statement]

nation. It is engaged in a divine calling. Even if this truth is not perceived, and the state carries out its work in a secular manner, this fact remains. All employment and those who enter into any part in the labor force are part of a holy field. It all belongs to our sovereign Lord. The Department of Labor in any country is evidence that those in government are made in the image of God.

CALL TO WORK

The concept of being "called" to a certain occupation may seem strange unless one is in some form of Christian ministry. Most of us work out of interest, need, or both, rather than from a sense of God's "calling."

By the end of the first chapter of Genesis we learn that Adam's work was neither from need nor desire, but resulted from the will of God. God called both Adam and Eve not only to work but also to a specific type of work.

> *Then God said, "Let us make man in our image, in our likeness, and let them rule over the fish of the sea and the birds of the air, over the livestock, over all the earth, and over all the creatures that move along the ground."*
>
> *So God created man in his own image, in the image of God he created him; male and female he created them. God blessed them and said to them, "Be fruitful and increase in number; fill the earth and subdue it. Rule over the fish of the sea and the*

> birds of the air and over every living creature that
> moves on the ground. "
>
> (GENESIS 1:26-28)

The Genesis passage provides more specifics about God's calling upon people to enter into work. God's calling to work is not a suggestion but a command (v. 28).

Later in Chapter 2 we learn what God specifically called Adam to do:

> The LORD God took the man and put him in
> the Garden of Eden to work it and take care of it.
>
> (v. 15)

Never did Adam or Eve need to worry about what they were to do regarding a job or a career. They were not to work in offices, but in the fields, orchards and barns. They were called to be farmers and ranchers in the Garden of Eden. There they had charge of caring for the beasts of the field, birds of the air and fruit-bearing plants. It is believed to have been a most beautiful and dynamic place to live and work. Although it took effort, it was not burdensome.

Their work was to follow the pattern set forth in Chapter 1. Adam was to name all the animals. The work of a farmer and rancher would take daily planning, gathering of resources, and properly using them. Some days I suspect the time was spent watching and caring for the newborn calf or lamb. Other days, perhaps, were spent planting, or, harvesting the fruit of an orchard. All these incredible resources were from and belonged to God. Everything and anything they needed was provided. It would, however, never belong to them except as stewards: He would retain the "title." He still holds the title to His universe. He still calls those made in His image to work.

What Adam and Eve experienced in the workplace has never been duplicated. It must have been a marvelous experience to live in a world untainted by sin. Because of the difficulties and hardships associated with work, we tend to assume that work itself must be a curse from God. Often that is how it is viewed and treated. Sin has had an ugly impact upon work. Genesis 3 informs us that the workplace would be characterized by conflict and pain because of the disobedience of Adam and Eve. At this point in time we only experience "work cursed."

As we have seen from the beginning of Genesis, work is actually a gracious gift and privilege from the sovereign Lord of the universe. We have been invited to join in a most sacred, holy task as we experience God's calling to be productive.

—— REFLECTION ——

What have you learned about work
from this chapter?

———

Do you consider work to be a *holy* area?

———

What difference should the Genesis view of
vocation make in your thinking and life?

———

Do you believe that God has called you
to your present job?
How does this affect your attitude
about your work?

———

Does God's work of creation challenge you
in the way you go about your job?
Please provide some specific examples.

———

How does your being created in the image of God
show in your work?

———

What are some of the characteristics of God that are
demonstrated in your work?

WORK EXCELLENCE

O LORD, *I give You praise for Your magnificent work of creation that I am able to enjoy. Indeed, the heavens do declare Your glory, O God, and the skies proclaim the work of Your hands. Help me to work for Your glory and praise. Give me the wisdom to understand what it means to work as one who was made in Your image and for Your glory! Amen*

CHAPTER 3

THE GOSPEL IN THE WORKPLACE

IN 1974 the Philippine government created its Overseas Employment Administration (POEA) to regulate and advance what is known worldwide as the Overseas Filipino Workers. The POEA has attempted to address the nation's high unemployment and foreign exchange problems. Those who find employment in other countries willingly separate themselves from families in the hope of providing a better standard of living for themselves and their loved ones.

My wife Debby and I met many Filipinos who were working overseas while ministering in the United Arab Emirates in the mid-1990s. They were attending a Bible study and worship service, which we led during our stay. Many served expatriates or Arabs as domestic workers. Saudi Arabia and similar places employed over one million such workers during the mid-1980s.

In the 1920s Filipino workers first came to the United States in significant numbers to work in the sugar and pineapple plantations of Hawaii. In time Filipino workers were employed on the East Coast, in such places as New York City. Not all of them had positive experiences. Sadly, abusive treatment of Filipino workers employed by Filipino-Americans has been reported. Writer Michael Matthews shared one such case:

> *Back in 1979, I had befriended a few Filipino domestic workers while working as a maintenance man on Roosevelt Island in New York City. I remember that during my two years of employment I had encountered a Filipino woman in her late 50's who happened to be working as a nanny and cook for a Filipino-American couple on the island.*
>
> *One day out of the blue the woman had confided in me about her personal work conditions. She told me that she was an undocumented alien without work authorization who was forced to work around the clock for seven days a week without a day off from work. Her wages were $50 a month while the minimum hourly wage at the time was about $1.75 an hour. She further stated that the Filipino doctor and his wife had taken her passport so that she could not leave them before she finishes her contract of employment.*

How does it feel to be treated abusively—as if a slave—within the workplace? Little could be more humiliating than to have one's dignity stripped away by a greedy employer. One need not be employed in a low-paying job to find life discouraging, however. There are many highly paid professionals who feel equally disheartened by their jobs. And I think it would be fair to say that there are also many employers and managers who feel cheated by the poor performance of those who work under them.

What should be a Christian's response to such circumstances? The apostle Paul's words, found in his letter to the believers in Ephesus, are timely:

> *Slaves, obey your earthly masters with respect and*
> *fear, and with sincerity of heart, just as you would*
> *obey Christ. Obey them not only to win their favor*
> *when their eye is on you, but like slaves of Christ,*
> *doing the will of God from your heart. Serve whole-*
> *heartedly, as if you were serving the Lord, not men,*
> *because you know that the Lord will reward every-*
> *one for whatever good he does, whether he is slave*
> *or free. And masters, treat your slaves in the same*
> *way. Do not threaten them, since you know that he*
> *who is both their Master and yours is in heaven,*
> *and there is no favoritism with him.*
>
> (EPHESIANS 6:5-9)

In Paul's day slavery was common in the Roman Empire. Some slaves were well educated and placed in responsible positions. In the last 2,000 years, even some Christians have found slavery acceptable. As late as the 19th century, some Christian theologians defended the right to own slaves as property. Abolition of slavery has been quite recent: in the United States of America it occurred in the mid-1800s.

People were enslaved for many reasons: nonpayment of debt, being citizens of a nation that had lost a war, or being a child of slaves. Paul did not intend to change the position in which his listeners found themselves. In his letter to Philemon, he does not condemn his friend for having a slave. He does, however, challenge those who are part of the church, whether free or slave, to understand what it means to be transformed by the gospel. Although slavery is rare today, Paul's exhortation does have important applications for those who have given their lives to Christ.

Paul calls us to examine two areas of life in the workplace: outward performance and the inner heart.

OUTWARD PERFORMANCE

Is it important for me to maintain a standard of excellence in my work? What criteria do I use in determining the standard? I have known people who felt satisfied with their day's work as long as they had looked busy for eight hours. At times I may be tempted to work in a way that is pleasing only to myself.

All of us work for someone. This is true for owners of companies or for presidents of nations. Some are under the immediate direction of a manager and others serve as supervisors who answer to a superior or to a board of directors. Even the person who is self-employed has to tailor his product or service to the standards of the customer.

Paul directs us to consider carefully the expectations of those for whom we work:

> *Obey your earthly masters with respect and fear...Obey them not only to win their favor when their eye is on you...*
>
> (EPHESIANS 6:5-6)

What does it mean to obey an earthly master with respect and fear? The person who performs well only when in the presence of the boss does not qualify.

To work under an employer or supervisor means that my performance at the end of the day must please him or her. His or her expectations become the standard for my job. To work with integrity means that I carry out the task in the spirit of my boss's directions. Also, I need to demonstrate a genuine interest in his or her will by being attentive to the directions and orders given.

We easily can imagine times when submitting to the will of a boss might be difficult. Our pride causes conflict here. We do not, in general, like to submit to anyone.

Careful understanding and execution of the task at hand is required. Outward performance alone, however, will not satisfy biblical standards of work excellence.

INNER HEART

In 1 Samuel we learn that the sons of Jesse lined up for Samuel to anoint one as King of Israel. The prophet dutifully was carrying out God's command. Faced with the challenge of deciding which son should be king, however, he looked at the outward appearance. In 1 Samuel we read:

> *Samuel replied, "Yes in peace; I have come to sacrifice to the LORD. Consecrate yourselves and come to the sacrifice with me." Then he consecrated Jesse and his sons and invited them to the sacrifice.*
>
> *When they arrived, Samuel saw Eliab and thought, "Surely the Lord's anointed stands here before the LORD." But the LORD said to Samuel, "Do not consider his appearance or his height, for I have rejected him. The LORD does not look at the things man looks at. Man looks at the outward appearance, but the LORD looks at the heart."*
>
> (1 SAMUEL 16:5-7)

According to the Scripture, the outward appearance, no matter how attractive, is only a part of the picture. God is concerned with the condition and integrity of the heart. A person may receive the loudest praise from men and, yet, if the heart lacks integrity, will never meet with God's approval.

Paul makes the same point here for anyone who works. No matter how well you please your supervisor or boss, you fall short of biblical excellence if your heart is not right. Consider verses 5 through 7 again:

> *Slaves, obey your earthly masters with respect and fear, and with* **sincerity of heart***, just as you would obey Christ. Obey them not only to win their favor when their eye is on you, but like slaves of Christ, doing the will of God* **from your heart***.*
>
> **Serve wholeheartedly***, as if you were serving the Lord, not men,*

Work done with sincerity of heart, or wholeheartedly, matches the will of God.

THE GOSPEL

Our obedience and service to Christ is the model we are to follow in serving our employers, supervisors or bosses.

How can we serve those for whom we work as though we were serving and obeying Christ? How <u>does</u> one obey Christ? How do we serve and please Him?

You might hear many suggestions from those who call themselves Christian. Some will instruct you to follow the way of discipline: knowing what is right, you dedicate yourself to following God's will. A life marked by obedience will bring and keep you in the favor of God. You willingly forfeit anything that might get in the way and cause you to be distracted. Discipline can be accomplished by one's own sincerity and determination.

Another suggestion for pleasing and obeying Christ is to follow biblical principles and steps. The Bible is often used to develop principles, rules and steps as a means of living life and pleasing God. Both approaches can lead to a mindset that Christianity is nothing more than a set of rules and formulas. The individual steps may not be wrong in themselves if they come from the Scriptures. When self-discipline, principles and rules are undertaken outside the context of the gospel and complete dependence on Christ, however, there is real trouble. In essence the person becomes his own savior. This is a form of paganism. Can the law give you life or save you? No. It shows you your need for Christ. Only Christ is the Savior. If we are to please Him, then He must enable us to do so. The apostle Paul understood this when he wrote about the importance of depending upon Christ in 2 Corinthians 12:

> To keep me from becoming conceited because of these surpassingly great revelations, there was given me a thorn in my flesh, a messenger of Satan, to torment me. Three times I pleaded with the Lord to take it away from me. But he said to me, "My grace is sufficient for you, for my power is made perfect in weakness." Therefore I will boast all the more gladly about my weaknesses, so that Christ's power may rest on me. That is why, for Christ's sake, I delight in weaknesses, in insults, in hardships, in persecutions, in difficulties. For when I am weak, then I am strong.
>
> (vv. 7-10)

Many Christians do not understand what it means to trust in Christ as they go about their daily lives. Some believe that although Christ has saved them from the penalty of sin, still it is up to them to live a life pleasing to God now that they are saved. They are often frustrated and difficult to be around. They have abandoned the gospel. We need Christ's finished work to be justified before God and we must trust Him for the continual process of growing in our faith. This includes our work.

Every day you need the Savior to work in your life in such a manner that you will outwardly and inwardly please your boss. The ability to follow the Scriptures with any degree of discipline will come from depending on Christ. We have no ability on our own to obey an earthly master with respect, fear and sincerity of heart, even though we may appear to outwardly. If on my own I can please God in this area, then of what value is Christ? I need Christ and His power. In weakness I go to Him, acknowledging my need for Him. When my work reflects this truth it will reflect my Lord's glory.

—— REFLECTION ——

What is your attitude towards
your employment and its environment
(the place and those with whom you work)?

———

Does it matter to you how you carry out
your responsibilities in your work? Why?

———

What person has had a significant influence
on your work habits and attitude?

———

Is your work done in the context of the gospel?
Please explain.

———

Do you ever try to be your own savior rather than
depending on Christ and His gospel? How does the
gospel impact your life at work?

———

What would you change about your job
or attitude towards it?

WORK EXCELLENCE

*L*ORD, at times I am tempted to work in such a manner that would please myself only. I want to be lord of the workplace. Show me when I do this. Enable me, by your grace, to see the lack of integrity and to serve others wholeheartedly, as one who works for You. May my service and accomplishments cause others to think of You. Amen.

CHAPTER 4

WORSHIP: CAIN & ABEL

FOR over twenty years our four children grew up in a church that provided great examples of what it means to love and worship God. Debby and I are extremely grateful to the Lord for giving our children such a wonderful church family in Oklahoma City. In this context they learned the importance of demonstrating love for God by worshipping Him through the giving of tithes and offerings.

At a young age our children observed their parents placing a tithe or gift in the offering plate. When they were two or three years old, they asked for pocket change so that they, too, could participate in that part of worship. I suspect that, at first, their requests were motivated by social pressure—children tend to model their parents. Eventually, though, they gave out of their own accounts (they gave a portion of their own allowances or money earned doing small jobs). I doubt that they understood the significance of what they were learning, that giving to God is no small thing.

As they grew, our children understood that their giving should be a portion of what they considered to be their own—a result of their own labor. They were learning that giving to God is costly and maybe even painful. This is a different dimension to the work issue.

What is the chief purpose of work? Do you work mainly to build up the greatest possible amount of wealth, so you can experience the greatest possible comfort in life? Believing that God calls you to your career or work is only a beginning step toward fully understanding all that His call includes for you. Knowing how to view and handle your income in a way that honors and worships God could be a greater challenge than you may have anticipated.

Genesis 4 challenges our understanding of the relationship between our work and worship. What is God's will regarding worshipping Him with our earned resources?

> *Adam lay with his wife Eve, and she became pregnant and gave birth to Cain. She said, "With the help of the LORD I have brought forth a man." Later she gave birth to his brother Abel. Now Abel kept flocks, and Cain worked the soil. In the course of time Cain brought some of the fruits of the soil as an offering to the LORD.*
>
> *But Abel brought fat portions from some of the firstborn of his flock. The LORD looked with favor*

on Abel and his offering, but on Cain and his offer-
ing he did not look with favor. So Cain was very
angry, and his face was downcast.

Then the LORD said to Cain, "Why are you
angry? Why is your face downcast? If you do what
is right, will you not be accepted? But if you do not
do what is right, sin is crouching at your door; it
desires to have you, but you must master It."

(GENESIS 4: 1-7)

What are we told about these two sons of Adam and Eve? We are not given any details of their lives as children. Nor are we given their ages. We are told of their births and occupations. Both sons studied agriculture. The younger of the two is mentioned first: his specialty was working with animals. The older son worked the soil. With the exception of their parents, they were the world's experts in their fields.

We would like to know how long they worked before the incident reported in this passage. Also, what did Cain grow? What kinds of herds, and how big, did Abel have? Why are we not told these things in the Bible? Perhaps our interest in the details would distract us from God's purposes in giving the account of Cain and Abel. We need to focus on what is given. The passage is about *their work as it relates to worship.*

What concerns do you have about your work? Many want to know that they will have some stability in their work, as well as receiving the promised benefits. Also, we anticipate that over time wages and benefits will increase. How often have you heard someone mention their anxiety about the impact their work has on their worship? Since leaving seminary in 1979, I never have had persons ask for counsel or encouragement because they were concerned about the influence their work was having on their worship.

THE CALL TO WORSHIP

When did Adam, Eve, or their children receive instructions for worship? We assume from the text that such direction had been given. We are told few other facts. The Law, along with the many details about how to worship, would not come for a long, long time, through Moses and the Israelites. Genesis 4 provides the limited amount of information we have about their understanding of worship.

First, it was expected and understood that what they considered theirs was not. This is a hard lesson. We all tend to be self-oriented when it comes to our property. Yet the person who belongs to God will learn that all that is in his possession does not belong to him. God holds the title to all that we have. Therefore, for Him to instruct us to release a portion for Himself is His "call." We are not told the size of the portion that the brothers were to offer. I suspect it had to be sizable. Cain gave some of the fruit of the soil. Abel gave some of the fat portions of the flock. There must be, in giving any offering, an element of sacrifice if it is to be worship.

When you consider what it takes to earn a living, how much will be enough? No matter how much you earn, as time progresses, you seem to need more. To some extent this is about contentment. We are tempted to define our happiness in the things that we want, yet do not have. We say to ourselves, "I will be happy when I have a new home, a loving spouse, children, the newer car or right vacation." This is evidence of idolatry. It is an acknowledgment that other things—anything besides God—will fulfill and make me content and happy. The other things will *never* make you happy. To be denied this pursuit of idolatry is a *blessing*. When offering God what pleases Him, we find a good sacrifice. Not only does it glorify Him, but it also restrains the evil of discontentment. Cain and Abel were being challenged to give in worship that which they might otherwise call their own. They needed this reminder.

Those who know and belong to Christ realize the importance of worship. Worship will take place for all eternity. Does it matter how we enter worship as long as the sacrifice is for the glory of God? From Genesis to Revelation we learn what does and does not please God when it comes to entering His presence.

In John 4, people went into shock when Christ conversed with a Samaritan woman at Jacob's well. He broke the social norms of the day. Their verbal exchange eventually came to the topic of worship. The Samaritan woman expressed her belief that the way she chose to worship God was acceptable. In response, Christ informed her why this was wrong.

"Sir," the woman said, "I can see that you are a prophet. Our fathers worshiped on this mountain, but you Jews claim that the place where we must worship is in Jerusalem." Jesus declared, "Believe

*me, woman, a time is coming when you will wor-
ship the Father neither on this mountain nor in
Jerusalem. You Samaritans worship what you do
not know; we worship what we do know, for salvation is from the Jews. Yet a time is coming and has
now come when the true worshipers will worship
the Father in spirit and truth, for they are the kind
of worshipers the Father seeks. God is spirit, and
his worshipers must worship in spirit and in truth."*

(JOHN 4: 19-24)

God does not accept just any form of worship, no matter the
sincerity of the worshipper. It must be done in spirit and in
truth—that is, worship must match God's standard. That
standard is absolute. This makes perfect sense. Why would the
God of the Bible take any and all forms of worship? This would
be inconsistent with all that we know about Him. What Christ
says here in the gospel was fundamentally what Cain understood. When God rebuked Cain He reminded him of what he
had been taught:

> *If you do what is right, will you not be accepted?
> But if you do not do what is right, sin is crouching
> at your door; it desires to have you, but you must
> master it.*

(GENESIS 4:7)

Cain knew, but refused to believe God, and went his own way. The text says, "In the course of time Cain brought some of the fruits of the soil as an offering to the LORD." (v.3)

The implication is that this was not the best of his labor, but was whatever he felt like giving. Perhaps he thought, "After all, God should be pleased with whatever He gets from us."

John, in his epistle, says this about Cain and his worship:

> *This is the message you heard from the beginning: We should love one another. Do not be like Cain, who belonged to the evil one and murdered his brother.*
>
> (I JOHN 3:11-12)

And why did he murder him? Because his own actions were evil and his brother's were righteous.

A congregation might be a bit shocked if their pastor called them evil for not giving proper tithes and offerings. Would such a response be an indication of the distance that exists between the present practice of worship and what Scriptures teach? The way we manage our income from work concerns God. Our worship is an indication of life's deeper issues. Cain showed no concern for God's position and, therefore, no repentance. His stingy worship was the tip of the wicked iceberg, which was exposed when he invited his brother into the workplace for a murder.

Abel's worship contrasts to his brother's:

> In the course of time Cain brought some of the
> fruits of the soil as an offering to the LORD. But
> Abel brought fat portions from some of the firstborn
> of his flock. The LORD looked with favor on Abel
> and his offering,
>
> (GENESIS 4:3-4)

Abel was not about to let unproductive time pass by. He worked hard caring for the flocks to have something to offer the Lord. Abel gave fat portions from the firstborn. He presented the best of his work, not the leftovers. He captured the essence of what God was calling him to pursue. He showed his position when it came to the worth of God. Abel desired to please God, and did. He is well thought of in the Scriptures, as demonstrated by the 11th chapter of Hebrews:

> Now faith is being sure of what we hope for and cer-
> tain of what we do not see. This is what the
> ancients were commended for. By faith we under-
> stand that the universe was formed at God's com-
> mand, so that what is seen was not made out of
> what was visible. By faith Abel offered God a better
> sacrifice than Cain did. By faith he was commend-
> ed as a righteous man, when God spoke well of his
> offerings. And by faith he still speaks, even though
> he is dead.
>
> (vv. 1-4)

Abel's work was very much tied to his faith. Did he see what was to come? Did he understand that his worship foreshadowed what was to come in Christ? An offering in itself is worthless if it is not tied to the gospel. The shepherd who brought the lamb as a sacrifice may not have fully understood what was being proclaimed in that act of worship. Yet the Scriptures teach that the offering was a picture of Christ's perfect life and sacrifice. For that reason the offering had to be the best.

There is no excellence in work if it does not lead to worship. It is a privilege to engage in an activity where you are productive. Your week at work and your worship are tied together. To have something to offer the Lord as result of your labor is an even greater honor. If worship is to please Him it must be done in concert with His character and will. This pleasing worship is possible only through Christ. He alone will enable you to worship in spirit and truth.

— REFLECTION —

What is your attitude
when it comes to worshipping God?

———

Do you view worship as an opportunity to
receive from or give to your Lord?

———

Are you usually aware that your work and
worship are closely related?

———

In your worship, do you look for ways to increase or
decrease your tithes and offerings?

———

Has this Genesis passage confirmed or challenged
your way of work and worship?

WORK EXCELLENCE

*M*OST *Holy and Sovereign Lord, You have blessed us with resources and abilities. You have called us to work in a manner that would result in greater ability to honor You in our worship. Help us to see and repent of any work or worship patterns that offend You. Show us by Your grace what it means to worship You in spirit and truth.*

Chapter 5

Conflict

HOW much do you enjoy your job? Many see work as a serious source of stress and conflict. You may be the exception, or you may know someone who always finds work enjoyable.

Work certainly was pleasant for Adam and Eve. For a significant season in their lives, they found work to be only good. The day came, however, when paradise ended. This lovely couple gave in to temptation. God's command was easily put aside when Satan presented his evil views. With an outstretched hand, the forbidden fruit was taken, and the clear order of God was laid aside by our parents.

Today the world laughs at anyone who declares such behavior "evil." The world's view is obviously foolish when we consider the degree of unhappiness and pain that resulted from Adam and Eve's actions. God considered the disobedience

horribly offensive. The third chapter of Genesis informs us of
the consequences of Adam and Eve's sin:

> *So the LORD God said to the serpent, "Because*
> *you have done this, "Cursed are you above all the*
> *livestock and all the wild animals! You will crawl*
> *on your belly and you will eat dust all the days of*
> *your life. And I will put enmity between you and*
> *the woman, and between your offspring and hers;*
> *he will crush your head, and you will strike his*
> *heel." To the woman he said, "I will greatly*
> *increase your pains in childbearing; with pain you*
> *will give birth to children. Your desire will be for*
> *your husband, and he will rule over you." To Adam*
> *he said, "Because you listened to your wife and ate*
> *from the tree about which I commanded you, 'You*
> *must not eat of it,' "Cursed is the ground because*
> *of you; through painful toil you will eat of it all the*
> *days of your life. It will produce thorns and thistles*
> *for you, and you will eat the plants of the field. By*
> *the sweat of your brow you will eat your food until*
> *you return to the ground, since from it you were*
> *taken; for dust you are and to dust you will return."*
>
> (GENESIS 3: 14-19)

Sometimes we have significant conflict in our work. For
some of us, work and conflict are synonymous—there is no
distinction. This passage describes the circumstances that
brought pain to the workplace. Yet, we learn more than simply

the circumstances: we learn here of the *necessity* and the *nature* of the conflict that we experience. This leaves us with a question: Is there any remedy to such conflict?

NECESSITY OF CONFLICT

In some ways this passage could cause considerable despair because of the bad news it brings.

Have you ever spent hours cleaning and preparing your home for guests, only to discover an hour before they arrive that your children or family pets have created a major mess? You know what it is like to have your work marred by the actions of others. The rebellion of this first couple did taint God's work of creation. The world functioned in a harmonious manner before Adam and Eve gave in to the serpent's will. Their sin, however, is only part of the reason that conflict exists in the world.

Life certainly was different after the forbidden fruit was eaten. Within a short while Adam and Eve were discontent not only with the will of God but with their own appearances as well. Fig leaves became the first designer clothing line. Until then there had been no need for clothing, no need to engage in the work of designing and manufacturing apparel (Genesis 3:7). When Adam and Eve heard God walking in the garden, they were no longer interested in pursuing Him; instead, they hid from their Maker (Genesis 3:8). When confronted with their disobedience, they insisted that they were not responsible for what they had done: it was someone else's fault (Genesis 3:12-13). Thus began the time of happiness lost.

The Genesis passage is disturbing in many respects. Why? Because it not only speaks about the impact of sin, but it also reveals the first hint and demonstration of God's anger. Life and work have become clouded by God's wrath.

I think the order of the following verses is important. The first thing God does is to inform Eve that henceforth there will be significant conflict in the world. God is not losing His temper but rather displaying His justice when He speaks of the spiritual warfare that exists and will be part of history.

And I will put enmity between you and the woman,
and between your offspring and hers.

(GENESIS 3: 15A)

Second, He informs Eve that her work in bearing children will be painful, and Adam will find the ground difficult to work. Life is going to be rough. Why? Because God's justice must be revealed. The Scripture is very clear that God is not just "stepping out" for a minute, and then bad things begin to happen. No, the Genesis 3 passage speaks about the deliberate actions of God. God said:

"I will greatly increase your pains in childbearing...
Cursed is the ground because of you; through
painful toil you will eat of it all the days of your life."

(vv. 16-17)

God is not making observations; He is pronouncing His judgment on creation. Bible students occasionally shy away from the wrath of God because it seems so unattractive. Some have difficulty reconciling it with His love, grace and mercy. But the Bible never apologizes for revealing it. In fact, it is the focus of the Old and New Testaments alike. Paul speaks about God's wrath throughout his epistles (letters). The most noteworthy demonstration of God's wrath is the judgment that Jesus Christ experienced in His life, suffering, and cruel death on the cross. In the garden of Gethsemane Christ specifically prayed about receiving God's wrath before being arrested, asking that, if possible, the cup be removed (Matthew 26:39). The "cup" is a reference to God's wrath (Jeremiah 25:15).

When you come home from work tired, worn out, and ready to quit, or when you find that weeds have taken over your garden, you are being reminded of God's judgment and wrath. For those who do not believe, it is an unheeded warning of what is to come.

THE NATURE OF CONFLICT

The things in life that should be so pleasant have become tainted with discomfort. The blessing of children is achieved through the difficult process of giving birth. The wonder and delight of engaging in creative God-like activity, such as baking bread, building a back yard fence, or erecting a 100-story office building, can bring a great deal of tension. At times things do not go as planned. The environment we live in is full of conflict. There is, however, a precise difference in the conflict relative to women and men.

God addressed Eve before Adam. Did she dread the divine exchange as a disobedient child who had been "caught in the act"? Perhaps she hoped God was going to turn the clock back and repair the damage instantly. Instead, she was confronted with words that had little or no meaning: There would be pain in childbirth. What was "pain"? Had she ever experienced it before? Discomfort, yes, in a sense. No longer was she comfortable with her outward appearance and the presence of God. But what was it to have pain in childbirth? This she would know in time. Why did God pick childbirth? How can we know?

What I do know is that I have seen the extent of the pain while witnessing our four children come into the world. Debby and I married in the winter of 1974 and the Lord has blessed us with Phillip, Katie, Anna and Peter. I have had the privilege of being with my wife during each birth. Sometimes the labor lasted over 13 hours. There were times when I found it difficult to watch. What was so amazing was the relatively short time that would pass before Debby was willing to do it all over again. A mother's work, as rewarding as it may be, includes its share of pain, from birth onward, even after the child leaves the home.

Adam was not to escape the difficulty of life's work. Perhaps at first he thought to himself, "She is in big trouble for giving me that forbidden fruit." Little did he know! He too would be held accountable for his disbelief and rebellion. The ground would no longer cooperate as it had before. From then on it would exist in a cursed state:

"Cursed is the ground because of you; through painful toil you will eat of it all the days of your life."

(v. 17b)

Life on the farm would be different now: to have the same harvest, considerably more time and effort would be required. Farming would be a struggle. Now Adam would find that new chores would need to be done repeatedly, weeding and hoeing.

Anyone who has gardened will tell you that it is constant work. In junior high school I worked for my grandfather, who grew Christmas trees. During the summer we trimmed and shaped each tree in preparation for the coming Christmas. In one section alone there were 10,000 trees to shape. The high weeds that occasionally hid black snakes needed constant cutting. The humid summers made it extremely uncomfortable to work.

My siblings and I spent summers weeding and hoeing the family garden. Did I like doing it? No. If you ask me why I have not enjoyed gardening, I would say that it is because I hate to weed. Every weed pulled and chopped is a reminder of the tragic day that Adam and his wife Eve decided to do life their way. Even more, each weed speaks of the righteous anger of God. That anger remains evident, even today.

Work, the great gift from God in which we are each called to take part, is often characterized by turmoil and tension. It comes with weeds and thistles. At times the weeds are too much for the farmer, or there is too much rain, or high winds destroy the crops. For the investor, it is a bad market or economy. For a schoolteacher, it may be a disruptive and undisciplined student. For a national senator, it is angry constituents. At other times the thistles may be bad relationships at work that never seem to be resolved. The weeds are numerous. Work is hard. If it is not the weeds, it is the tensions that exist between fellow workers. Please, somebody, help!

HOPE

In the passage there is also the message of hope. We find here a reference to the gospel. For those who have surrendered their lives to Christ in repentance and faith, the garden thorns are a reminder of the reality of the hope of heaven.

God curses Satan and reveals to him that the day will come when the seed of the woman will deliver the final and fatal blow to him: "he will crush your head" (Genesis 3:15). This refers to the impact of Christ's death and resurrection upon the evil deceiver.

The pain associated with children, or the sharp sting experienced when pulling the garden thistle, is a foreshadowing of the hell to come. In referring to God's wrath, Paul says,

> *They tell how you turned to God from idols to serve the living and true God, and to wait for his Son from heaven, whom he raised from the dead— Jesus, who rescues us from the coming wrath.*

(I THESSALONIANS 1:9b-10)

Paul speaks about the sure hope that belongs to those who, by faith, have experienced God's reconciliation through Christ. The pain and discomfort are temporal. This is the great message of the gospel. If there is no stabbing pain in childbirth or no thistle injury, then there is no gospel. The gospel has no meaning without recognition of the pain from sin that ignites the anger of God. Our hope is in Christ alone, not in the absence of pain.

Christ brings eternal life to those who believe. When we were counted as enemies (Romans. 5:10), He reconciled us to the Father. He brings comfort to those suffering in various ways (2 Corinthians 1:3-4); yes, even in the workplace. That same work of reconciliation can take place in an office known for its low morale and gossip. The same is true among political leaders of different parties or countries. Christ is the answer to a world in need. Those who cry out to this Savior will be heard!

— REFLECTION —

How do you characterize your job
and its environment?
Are you happy in your work? Please explain.

———

What are the "thistles" that exist
within your work?

———

Are there relationships at your place of
employment that need to be addressed with
grace and forgiveness? Please provide details.

———

How do you typically handle conflict and stress
at your place of employment?

———

Do you find the gospel relevant to the issues
at work? Does it make a difference?

WORK EXCELLENCE

L ORD, we often rationalize and defend our offenses towards You, as did our parents, Adam and Eve. Please forgive us when we ignore Your word and its clear commands. Please help us understand the significance of the pain and thistles of life, especially the hardships within our work. May our Savior Christ renew our work for Your glory.

Chapter 6

Joseph

I PROBABLY have never met a more conscientious worker than Jerry. Few men in my youth left as lasting an impression on me.

Jerry worked for a small group of German masons as a laborer. This African American man, who daily drove to work in the country from his inner city home in Baltimore, must have been at least sixty years old at the time. Two things about him impressed me.

First, he could outwork men many years younger than himself. He set up scaffolding, mixed and carried mortar, and hauled the bricks and blocks used by the masons. On long, hot summer days he ran from one place to another to satisfy his employer's needs. He gave them every bit of his strength.

Second, I remember his boldly praising Jesus Christ for his life and work. While it was acceptable at work to swear and curse, even to take the name of the Lord in vain, publicly praising the Savior resulted in disdain and insults. Dependent on Christ, Jerry knew the value of hard and diligent work. He exalted Christ in his life even though many had no appreciation for it.

In many ways Jerry reminds me of a man in the Old Testament named Joseph. We learn the details of his life in the last thirteen chapters of Genesis. The 39th chapter informs us of a difficult time in his life:

> *Now Joseph had been taken down to Egypt. Potiphar, an Egyptian who was one of Pharaoh's officials, the captain of the guard, bought him from the Ishmaelites who had taken him there. The LORD was with Joseph and he prospered, and he lived in the house of his Egyptian master. When his master saw that the LORD was with him and that the LORD gave him success in everything he did, Joseph found favor in his eyes and became his attendant. Potiphar put him in charge of his household, and he entrusted to his care everything he owned. From the time he put him in charge of his household and of all that he owned, the LORD blessed the household of the Egyptian because of Joseph. The blessing of the LORD was on everything Potiphar had, both in the house and in the field. So he left in Joseph's care everything he had;*

*with Joseph in charge, he did not concern himself
with anything except the food he ate.*

(GENESIS 39: 1-6B)

Joseph was forced to live and work in most difficult circumstances. Here, in Genesis, we see both the integrity of Joseph's work and the reasons behind such integrity.

Joseph was the younger and favored son of Jacob. Along with his many brothers, he lived in Canaan, sandwiched between the Jordan River and the Mediterranean Sea. As a young man of 17, Joseph and his brothers were given the responsibility of caring for their father's livestock. You could say that they worked in the family business. It was a sizable herd and needed large areas for grazing. Two other things about Joseph should be mentioned. He was known by his family to have abnormal dreams that implied that one day he expected to be in an exalted position over his family. Second, his brothers hated him. They despised their brother for being favored by their father.

One day Joseph was asked by his father to go to Shechem to check on his brothers and to report back. For Jacob to send Joseph to check on his brothers was a serious mistake. When he finally caught up to them, they had already agreed to use the occasion to take his life. If it had not been for elder brother Reuben, the young man would have died. Although Reuben also disliked Joseph, he knew what the act of hate would do to his father, Jacob. Reuben convinced his brothers to place Joseph into a cistern, with the hope that he might later return the younger brother to his father. While Reuben was gone, however, the others sold Joseph to Ishmaelite slave traders. They took Joseph to Egypt and sold him to Potiphar, one of Pharaoh's officials.

This new chapter in Joseph's life brought new challenges. He now lived and worked in the house of the Egyptian captain-of-the-guard. Joseph labored alongside many other slaves who cared for the house and fields. We cannot be certain of the exact responsibilities that he was given at first. We assume that that he did typical domestic work: cleaning, watering, and gardening. He slept in slave quarters and ate slave food. He was, for all practical purposes, a prisoner. Over time, the quality of his work won the trust of Potiphar, leading to significant promotions. Joseph became Potiphar's personal attendant, and was placed in charge of the entire estate. This slave became the master of Potiphar's household and all his possessions. The only thing not under his care was the food eaten by Potiphar. Why such an honored position? Both the quality of his work as well as the success and blessings that followed Joseph indicated that the Lord was with this Hebrew slave.

If we did not know better, we might think that Joseph was won over by his new position and home. Did he, perhaps, enjoy the cultural differences and prefer it to his home back in Canaan? We know that this was not the case. This chapter of his life was difficult, marked with suffering and trouble (Gen. 41:50-52). Work, under the best of circumstances, can be difficult. When forced to live in a foreign land and work for a stranger, his life worsened. Potiphar's wife falsely accused the trusted slave of attempted rape. Joseph's reward for the years of faithful and successful service was a prison sentence. Any cause for complaints as a slave now paled in comparison to being a prisoner in a damp dungeon. Yet even prisoners work. What do we know about the integrity of Joseph's work in prison?

In the latter portion of chapter 39 we find that Joseph's work, whatever it was, won him the favorable attention and trust of the warden. The convicted slave was placed in charge of the entire prison. The warden, as had Potiphar, entrusted everything to Joseph's oversight. What could possibly cause this man who had been treated with such injustice for so many years to exemplify work excellence? Certainly it was not the food!

REASON FOR EXCELLENCE

Scripture does not tell us specifically why Joseph worked with such integrity. His work excellence, I believe, resulted from several factors. We know that he grew up in a strong family. What had Joseph witnessed as a child? He would never have seen people sitting around with nothing to do but receive government welfare checks. If a person were not productive he could not eat, and, in time, he would die. Although known as a deceiver, Jacob was productive with his time and resources. He was a rancher with a degree of wealth and a large family. Everyone in the clan was expected to contribute his or her fair share and to do it with integrity. In other words, social pressure influenced Joseph's attitude and performance when it came to work. This influence also bore fruit after his relocation to Egypt. This reminds us that one of the means the Lord has created and uses to develop His calling to work is the family. But

that still does not tell us why Joseph was able to do so well
under such difficult and troubling circumstances.

Chapter 39 repeatedly mentions the presence of the Lord
within Joseph's life and work:

> *The Lord was with Joseph and he prospered....*
>
> *When his master saw that the Lord was with
> him and that the Lord gave him success inevery-
> thing he did....*

(vv. 2-3)

Think about this picture. The man is hated by his brothers
and sold into slavery. He now is a prisoner and forced to work,
eat, and live in a place not of his choosing. Would you consider such circumstances a picture of blessing? Most of us find our
mood negatively changed if someone imposes upon us, with
rudeness, at the grocery checkout line, much less selling us
into slavery. This is not what most would consider a blessing
from God. Yet, there is no question that it was a blessing.
Blessing is not defined by what we think we should have. God's
presence is always a blessing, even under the most difficult of
circumstances. It is God's nature to be gracious and faithful.
The English translation LORD is from the most sacred Hebrew
name of God, Yahweh. The name reveals God as one who
keeps His covenant and bestows grace upon His people; that is,
He is a God of blessing. If the Lord is present, then there is
blessing. The larger question is, Did Joseph know this?

It is evident that Joseph knew that God had not abandoned
Him, and he had no thoughts of abandoning his faith in God.

How did Potiphar know that the Lord was with Joseph? Perhaps any answer is speculative. However, if Potiphar knew anything about this covenant-keeping God, it was because the Hebrew slave had spoken about Him. Second, as the slave master saw the slave's faith at work, he perceived that it was more than words. The passage tells us that Potiphar saw that the Lord was with Joseph. We are not given the details of what Potiphar saw. Perhaps he observed that the work was not only done well and in a timely manner, but that it was fruitful: the flocks remained healthy and multiplied. Was the harvest abundantly more plentiful under this Hebrew slave? Did the other slaves work harder and longer under Joseph's management? Whatever it was, the master was very impressed with the slave and his God. Eventually the faith of this man would have an even greater impact upon this pagan nation.

Another point should be mentioned about Joseph's faith. It is evident that he had an enduring faith that persevered. The abuse from older brothers easily could have killed the faith of many. A sentence of slavery with no hope of freedom, along with being falsely accused of rape, would have been more than enough to cause most of us to stop trusting in God. "Who needs God if this is the reward I get for believing in Him?" one might be tempted to declare. And yet, what we see with Joseph is that his faith was not at all based on his circumstances. That is a radical concept. If Joseph had been depressed, angry, and moody, his witness would have been very different. He could easily have abused his position and trust, but he did not. Truly this is a picture of faith at work.

Revealing the presence of the Lord in our world is powerful and transforming. We wonder at the impact Joseph had upon the other slaves. What happens today in the workplace is important because it touches many others. A Christian who daily recognizes the presence of Christ in all of life will have a transforming impact upon others. The workplace is in desperate need of the gospel. Joseph provides for us a glowing example of such a witness. It is a picture of work excellence.

— REFLECTION —

As you consider Joseph's life,
what impact does it have on you?

____

What have you learned about excellence
in work from the life of Joseph?

____

How is your faith impacted when you find life and
work clouded by unfavorable circumstances?

____

What degree of respect and trust do you have
among those with whom you work?
Please explain.

____

How do you reveal the presence of God
in your life and place of work?

____

How important is your reputation
when it comes to your work?

____

How does the gospel impact your life in this area?

WORK EXCELLENCE

*L*ORD, thank You for my job. Thank You for those with and for whom I work. Please help me to understand what it means to live my life in Your presence. I know that the gospel is always at work in my life. Help me, by Your grace, to see the sin in my life and to experience, through Christ, Your forgiveness. Help me keep my eyes upon my Savior, especially when it comes to my work. May all that I do bring You glory.

Chapter 7

Calling

W ASHINGTON, DC, is a dynamic place to live, with
nearly every culture in the world represented. I
have sat in the same room with those who hold positions of
enormous power, and minutes later walked by a man who eats
and sleeps on city streets. Riding the Metro (mass transporta-
tion system) affords me the opportunity to meet many of the
District's residents.

One day, I boarded a bus near Dupont Circle and took the
empty seat next to a man who appeared to be in his twenties.
His father lived in Swaziland in southern Africa. His step-
mother worked in DC for USAID. My bus friend told me that,
for now, he worked for a well-known financial broker. This was
not his ultimate career goal, however. After putting in long
days at work, he would go home and study until midnight for
his entrance examination for graduate school. His career goals

were well-defined, and nothing was going to interfere with his achieving them. He had no question about what he would do as a career.

How does a person know exactly what type of work he or she should pursue? God calls each of us to work, but how do we know exactly what that work should be? For many of us this is a difficult question to answer. I see my own children wrestling with this problem.

We have said that God is the One who created us and called us to work. To enter into the workplace, wherever that might be, is to enter a holy place. While the Scriptures may not direct one to a specific job, what it says about work itself will be of enormous help in the search.

THE WILL OF GOD

The prophet Jeremiah warned the people of Jerusalem during the reigns of Kings Josiah, Jehoiakim, and Zedekiah of the coming destruction. When the warning was concluded he began his prayer with the following:

> *"I know, O LORD, that a man's life is not his own;*
> *it is not for man to direct his steps."*
>
> (JEREMIAH 10:23)

Although Jeremiah was not praying about people knowing the will of God regarding their work, his prayer reminds us that the Lord holds title to all that we are and have. Everyone who belongs to God will want Him to direct every area of our lives, including our choice of work. Every part of our lives needs to be examined in prayer before God, including the details of our work.

Many times we read about the need to pray and pursue the will of God. When we use the Lord's Prayer (Matthew 6:9-13), we say in the third petition, "Your kingdom come, your will be done on earth as it is in heaven." In their letters, both the apostles Paul and Peter frequently directed their readers to be concerned with the will of God (Romans 1: 10; 8:27; 15:32; 2 Corinthians 8:5; 1Peter 2:15). How, then, are we to discern His will?

First, we acknowledge that God has made His will clear by speaking to us through His Word. God has been clear about His will for our relationships with Him and with other persons in this world. Guidelines regarding what we should think and do, as well as what we should not think and do, are plain. If I become dissatisfied with my wife and want to leave her, I am instructed in the Word of God to remain faithful: That is God's will. If you have offended me, and I want to take your life in revenge, God's will is clear: I am to love you instead. There is no mystery here. God reveals His will by speaking to us through the Scriptures. Yes, understanding the Bible may be challenging at times; however, those passages are few. My relationships with my wife, children, parents, church, community and world are addressed frequently in the Old and New Testaments. God has addressed a significant portion of our lives without us asking.

Second, we recognize that God is sovereign and, therefore, His will, as understood by His decrees and plan of redemption, is never altered. Redemptive history has taken place exactly as our Lord has decreed and directed. Nothing small or large takes place outside His total control. There are no battles with Satan that God loses. God's will always comes to completion. Nothing can rob God of His will, not even my sin and disobedience.

Do we live our lives knowing that it is God, and not we ourselves, who determines the outcome? We may disobey our Lord and thereby suffer the consequences; but we will never control or alter His sovereign will. As Joseph said to his evil brothers in Genesis 50:20, "You intended to harm me, but God intended it for good to accomplish what is now being done, the saving of many lives." God's perfect will was being carried out even though it may have appeared at times that it was being redirected.

While thinking about occupation or career we should keep in mind that God has given us discretion and freedom in many areas of our lives. When I get dressed I am not worried that my shirt and pants will be challenged by the will of God. If I want to eat eggs instead of fruit for breakfast, then I may decide as I please. I know the certainty of the Lord's will in this matter after I have completed my breakfast. Many areas in our lives are left to our discretion. Yes, we still pray that the Lord would guide and direct us; yet, when His Word is silent on an issue, we understand we have permission to go in whatever direction we choose. His silence on an issue is not a mistake.

God's sovereignty and will are often shown through our circumstances.

When Christians serve in the Body of Christ, we speak of them using their spiritual gifts. God gives us certain gifts and abilities that are from the working of the Holy Spirit (see Ephesians 4). Often these gifts are recognized by the individuals and others within the fellowship. The members will gravitate to the areas within the church that they have a desire for and in which they feel capable of serving. Their backgrounds and service will confirm where the Lord wants them. Some may care for children in the nursery; others may enter ministry as teaching pastors. To some degree this is true for the person seeking his or her place in the world of work. Life circumstances play a part in discerning God's will.

By the time a person has finished his or her schooling, many things will have taken place that will influence work or career choice. Family and culture will be a part of his or her makeup. He or she will have developed certain interests and experiences, and shown some giftedness, talents and abilities. The desire for certain types of work should not be ignored. This background, along with the options for work available, should be seen as from the Lord. It is an indication of His provision and will for our lives. One's family in Christ will, perhaps, see indications of what one's career should be by noting interests. Church counsel is not the word of God, but it may be an indication of where the Lord is leading.

Seeking God's guidance in this area is vitally important. Being in the wrong place of work can be very difficult and discouraging. Care should be taken to seek the Lord. Does He care? Our Lord is neither asleep nor still in the grave. He is alive and sits at the right hand of throne of God. He, too, is interceding for us before the throne of grace. Are you having difficulty with the issue of work? Do you need help and guidance? Your Lord and Redeemer is poised to help those who are in need. Only go to Him to receive guidance and assurance.

— REFLECTION —

What means do you generally use to
discern the Lord's will?

———

Do you believe that God has called you into a
specific type of work and place of employment?

———

How did you choose the type of work
or career you are in right now?

———

What does it mean for God to be sovereign over every
area of life, including our work?
What implications does God's sovereignty
have for your life?

———

Is it possible for you to change careers
or work and remain in the will of God?

WORK EXCELLENCE

*L*ORD, thank You for being totally in control of every aspect of life. You are the one who holds title to all of life. We acknowledge that it is easy to pursue life on our own and never seek You or Your will. Please guide us in our work and careers. Enable us to use those gifts and talents that are from You and are to be used for Your glory. Amen.

CHAPTER 8

WARNING: IDOLATRY

IT was the summer of 1982. We returned home after attending the wedding of a close friend in Los Angeles. The flight lifted out of LAX and headed northeast for Salt Lake City. Debby sat on one side of me, and a man we had never met sat on the other. Apparently close to retirement age, he presented himself as very self-sufficient and successful. He also was quite talkative; a few questions were all he needed to keep the conversation going for hours.

As we talked about him and his views, the conversation quickly centered on his work. For him, work was everything. His philosophy was simple: "Work is the most important part of life, and everything else must be subservient to it, including your family." I am positive that nothing ever came before work in his organization. In this regard my flight companion echoes the thinking of many down through the centuries.

In the gospel of Mark we read about a man who had a similar life and work philosophy:

> As Jesus started on his way, a man ran up to him and fell on his knees before him. "Good teacher," he asked, "what must I do to inherit eternal life?" "Why do you call me good?" Jesus answered. "No one is good—except God alone. You know the commandments: 'Do not murder, do not commit adultery, do not steal, do not give false testimony, do not defraud, honor your father and mother.'" "Teacher," he declared, "all these I have kept since I was a boy." Jesus looked at him and loved him. "One thing you lack," he said. "Go, sell everything you have and give to the poor, and you will have treasure in heaven. Then come, follow me." At this the man's face fell. He went away sad, because he had great wealth.
>
> Jesus looked around and said to his disciples, "How hard it is for the rich to enter the kingdom of God!"
>
> (MARK 10: 17-23)

Luke 18 and Matthew 19 cover the same conversation. This young, wealthy businessman is referred to as a ruler in Luke's account, not because he was a king or governor, but because he had many under his authority. He may have owned a great deal of property. He was Jewish and would have been well-known in his community as a leader and businessman. Most communities have such men.

Microsoft's Bill Gates might be a contemporary parallel. This multibillionaire certainly has been in charge of many in his successful computer software business. Mr. Gates drives whatever car he chooses and lives in houses that most of us cannot even begin to imagine. He draws the attention of everyone: When he speaks, people listen. If he shows interest in some business venture, investors think that it must be a winner—and who would not want to invest in a winner? The world and its media are captivated by this kind of intoxicating power. Having "the world," however, does not mean that you have everything. This is clear from the details in Mark's gospel.

The manner in which the ruler approached Jesus probably drew the attention of those present. He anxiously hurried as he ran to Christ and dropped on his knees. Few approached Christ in that manner. It appeared as though he had lost all sense of dignity as a societal leader. Imagine the president of a nation or a Bill Gates doing the same. The young ruler was not content. The question, posed without any formal or informal introduction, accented the urgency. The issue was not physical or business-related. The man did not need healing. He was bothered because it had occurred to him that he was not prepared to die. All his life everything had seemed to be in order. Life had run according to his dictates. Is it possible that someone had been talking about the teachings of Jesus to this man, and it troubled him? He realized that all seemed fine except the spiritual. "Good teacher," he asked, "What must I do to inherit eternal life?" Why would a relatively young man concern himself with what happens after death? He needed the answer immediately.

SPIRITUALLY MINDED

Spiritual matters were not new to this Hebrew man. We can only speculate as to what caused this concern for matters spiritual. He had come to get the answer so that he could fix the problem and move on to his next burning issue. There were, undoubtedly, deals to be made and management decisions to direct. He knew that things are easily resolved if you bring in an expert. There was no question that Jesus was the right man for the job!

At first, he seemed confident that he could handle Jesus' answer. As Jesus established common ground with the Jewish leader, He began to answer the question:

> You know the commandments: 'Do not murder, do not commit adultery, do not steal, do not give false testimony, do not defraud, honor your father and mother.' "Teacher," he declared, "all these I have kept since I was a boy."
>
> (vv. 19-20)

The rich young ruler's response reflects both his knowledge of and respect for the Ten Commandments. In his mind he had always kept the Law. I have met others who would answer similarly. If a person believes that he has kept the law perfectly, then there is a real problem. The person is deceived and not well-connected to spiritual reality. Paul says in Romans 3:23, "For all have sinned and fall short of the glory of God." The person who says he has not sinned is a liar (I John 1:8-10). Christ does not confront him with his self-deception at this point. He moves on to the bigger issue:

> *Jesus looked at him and loved him. "One thing you lack," he said. "Go, sell everything you have and give to the poor, and you will have treasure in heaven. Then come, follow me." At this the man's face fell. He went away sad, because he had great wealth.*
>
> (vv. 2 I -2 2)

He had been so hopeful: This encounter was supposed to resolve his most significant issue. But he left without hope. What could be more tragic than to leave the presence of God in despair? To whom can we turn, if not to God? But then, there was the problem! The young ruler had not turned to God; He had come to Jesus as a "good teacher," and nothing more. Jesus addressed this first:

> *"Why do you call me good?" Jesus answered. "No one is good—except God alone."*
>
> (v. 18)

By not acknowledging the deity of Christ, this desperate man had completely misunderstood Christ's identity! In fact, the man had never recognized the presence of God. When

Christ asked him about following the law, he purposely quoted from the second half of the commandments, which concern our relationships with each other. Jesus addressed the first part of the law when He instructed him to sell his possessions, give to the poor, and follow Him. The Lord placed His holy finger on the hardened heart of idolatry.

Christ calls us to repent from lives so committed to work and all that it produces, that we have turned work into a god. If we work for anything other than God's glory, we worship the creation rather than the Creator.

The young man left the exchange disappointed, having been shown the truth. There would be no quick fix. He had worked hard and enjoyed its rewards. While many would see him as a picture of work excellence, he had ignored certain portions of the Bible. Idolatry is embracing things of the world as a means of giving us life, making us happy. This man had made his work and its benefits his source of happiness. When Christ revealed this to him he left in sadness. Christ was not teaching salvation by works. He wanted the rich, young ruler to see his sin and its evil. No one can go in two different directions at the same time. No one can please two different masters. He will love the one and hate the other. The ruler needed to repent of his idolatry and trust in Christ.

We believe, according to the Scriptures, that God has called us to work for His glory. We are to be faithful, diligent, and productive in our work. It is universally expected that productivity yields benefits. You will be paid a day's wage for a day's work. In some cases the rewards can be sizable and intoxicating. Those who apply themselves in their work must recognize the potential danger of their "calling from God" becoming their tool for dishonor. I dishonor the Lord when I allow my work to give me meaning, happiness and life. In some cases this may not be because of the wealth that I accumulate, but the glory and power of the position I hold. Every person who acquires a position of leadership in a city, state, or country lives with this danger. Even the disciples at times seemed to find the power of position tempting. The mother of James and John, the sons of Zebedee, came to Jesus requesting that her sons sit on His right and left (Mathew 20:20-22). Even though their mother made the request, I suspect they agreed with its presentation. There is no evidence of their objection. She wanted them to have an exalted position in the kingdom. When we find that we must have a certain position within our world in order to be satisfied, that, too, is sin.

No matter how good a job you do, there is no excellence in work when idolatry and sin are present. How can we benefit from the warning provided to the rich, young ruler? Being aware of this potential danger will help. Remember, you could find yourself so captivated by your work and what it gives you that it controls your life. Before long you have fallen into a pit of work worship. Second, if you think you may have already crossed the line or be moving towards it, why not ask a close friend for his or her evaluation? Others often see things long before we do. Finally, seek the Lord in prayer. The Lord's Prayer instructs us to petition our heavenly Father to protect us from temptation. There is good reason to make such a request: we are helpless to deal with life without our Savior, Christ. Our hope in avoiding all temptations is in Him, alone.

—— REFLECTION ——

"I will never need to worry about turning
my work into a tool for idolatry."
Is this statement <u>true</u> or <u>false</u> for you?

——

Who do you know that would fit
into the same category as a rich young ruler?
How do you see his or her life and work?

——

Would you warn a friend whom you knew
was making his/her career his source of life and happiness? What would you say to that friend?

——

What does it look like for you to depend upon
Christ and His gospel for life and happiness?

WORK EXCELLENCE

*L*ORD, show me the sin in my life in such a manner that I, too, can see the extent of my offense. Protect me from using the privilege of work as a tool for idolatry. May I work so as to bring You glory and not demean Your name.

Chapter 9

Rest

O N May 20, 1927, a crowd of 500 lined Roosevelt Field on Long Island to watch the making of history. The Spirit of St. Louis lifted off the rain-soaked runway for Paris. Thirty-three and one-half hours, and 3,500 miles later, Charles Lindbergh circled past the Eiffel Tower as he made his approach to land at Le Bourget Aerodrome.

A 33-½ hour flight presented many challenges in that period of aviation history. Before taking off he had been awake for 23 hours. This lack of rest proved to be the most difficult and dangerous factor of his flight. By 4 pm, less than nine hours after taking off, he found it difficult to stay awake. He later described this struggle:

There comes a point when the body's demand for sleep is harder to endure than any other pain I have encountered, when it results in a state of semi-consciousness in which an awareness exists that is less acute but apparently more universal than that of the normal mind. Before my flight was halfway finished, I found that I could not force myself to stay awake through will power. The rational mind I had previously known and relied upon had less and less effect on my body's responses. There were lengthening periods when it even lost the knowledge of its own existence, when intelligence without the need for reason had replaced it....

It was the only occasion in my life when I saw and conversed with ghosts. They appeared suddenly in the tail of the fuselage while I was flying through fog. I saw them clearly although my eyes were staring straight ahead. Transparent, mist like, with semi-human form, they moved in and out through the fabric walls at will. One or two of them would come forward to converse with me and then rejoin the group behind. I can still see those phantoms clearly in memory, but after I landed at Paris I could not remember a single word they said.[1]

Although I never have experienced Charles Lindbergh's level of sleep deprivation, my wife can tell you that living with me when I am overtired is challenging. No one disputes the importance of rest. The amount may vary, but we all need it.

---

1. Charles A. Lindbergh, *Autobiography of Values*, ed William Jovanovich, coed, Judith A. Schiff New York and London: Harcourt Brace Jovanovich (1978), pp. 11-12

There is another aspect of rest that the Bible speaks about: this is the Sabbath, or the Lord's Day.

When considering the Lord's Day, we think of what is said in the moral law, or Ten Commandments:

> *Remember the Sabbath day by keeping it holy. Six days you shall labor and do all your work, but the seventh day is a Sabbath to the LORD your God. On it you shall not do any work, neither you, nor your son or daughter, nor your manservant or maidservant, nor your animals, nor the alien within your gates. For in six days the LORD made the heavens and the earth, the sea, and all that is in them, but he rested on the seventh day. Therefore the LORD blessed the Sabbath day and made it holy.*
>
> (EXODUS 20:8-11)

There has been much discussion regarding the importance of Christians taking seriously the Lord's Day as a day of rest and worship. It is difficult to develop a biblical view of work excellence and not consider what is said regarding rest. If we ignore the day of rest, are we not only going against God's commandment, but also ignoring the nature of His work of creation? How can we be attentive to what He says about work and not to what He has said about the need to rest from work? The very beginning of God's revelation, reflected in the Exodus 20 passage, addresses what took place at the finish of creation:

Thus the heavens and the earth were completed in all their vast array. By the seventh day God had finished the work he had been doing; so on the seventh day he rested from all his work. And God blessed the seventh day and made it holy, because on it he rested from all the work of creating that he had done.

(GENESIS 2: 1-3)

Here we are told that creation was complete: The work of God had a beginning and an end. The ending ushered in a period of time in which there would be a specific rest in relation to work. That rest would take place on the seventh day and be distinctly set apart, made holy. God does not need to rest. In every way He is without limit. He is never exhausted. The rest was not because He needed a break in order to regain His strength and carry on creating another universe. The principle of a holy day was given before the sin of Adam and Eve; it was not a result of the Fall.

God has created nature to include the Sabbath. Even the land and animals need rest, as seen in Exodus 23. All that God has made, therefore, requires breaks from normal activities:

For six years you are to sow your fields and harvest the crops, but during the seventh year let the land lie unplowed and unused. Then the poor among your people may get food from it, and the wild animals may eat what they leave. Do the same with your vineyard and your olive grove. Six days do your work, but on the seventh day do not work, so that your ox and your donkey may rest and the slave born in your household, and the alien as well, may be refreshed.

(EXODUS 23: 10-12)

According to the Exodus passage, the land, the animals, the poor and the servants would benefit from rest. All are very different from God in that they do not have infinite energy to continually produce without rest. The land and animals will stop producing if they have no time to replenish. I have visited places such as Haiti where the land has been abused. Over time it wasted away and the people have suffered as a result. In a way, the person who does not rest cheats those for whom they work. They cannot be efficient and capable if they do not have a healthy break. As illustrated by Charles Lindbergh, we cannot go forever without experiencing some form of disturbance.

BECOMING A SLAVE TO CREATION

Are there other consequences of a lack of rest? Eventually the person becomes a slave to creation. He or she, in effect, will eventually serve a slave master that will seem all-consuming. People may work seven days a week to make more money or gain a promotion. Some never feel as though they can stop since the need for work never seems to cease. What are we to make of those who are dominated and consumed by creation? Do you remember what was said to Adam and Eve after they were created in the image of God?

So God created man in his own image, in the image
of God he created him; male and female he created
them. God blessed them and said to them, "Be
fruitful and increase in number; fill the earth and
subdue it. Rule over the fish of the sea and the birds
of the air and over every living creature that moves
on the ground."

(GENESIS 1:27-28)

Today the creation often rules over man. People are so
enamored with what the creation can give them that they are
willing to submit to its power. As in Romans 1, Paul has said:

They exchanged the truth of God for a lie, and wor-
shiped and served created things rather than the
Creator—who is forever praised. Amen.

(V.25)

It is easy to bow the knee to creation. To conclude your
week of work with a day of rest and worship states that your
attitude about work is consistent with that of the Scriptures.

When there is no rest there is little, if any, worship. The
Lord's Day is more than a time to stop working. It is a time to
rest from your work and a time to bring before the Lord the
fruit of your work. Is not the act of bringing your work to a stop
in itself an act of proper worship?

PRICE TO PAY?

If you think that adopting a biblical view in this area is without cost, think again. For the most part, the world is less likely to sustain a day of rest and worship than ever before. Businesses are much more oriented towards being open every possible day and hour. Why, they wonder, should they miss out on sales that will go to others? Maintaining a day of rest can cause considerable tension.

I felt this tension when a student in high school and university. As a young Christian I desired to honor the Lord in every area of my life. Reading the Scriptures convinced me that the Lord's Day was, for me, a time to put aside study. School was my work. It became my weekly habit not to prepare for my classes on that day. I had to do my homework before or after Sundays. Sometimes I rose early on Monday mornings to complete work before going to class. With few exceptions I was able to maintain this schedule without a great deal of conflict. High school and university were manageable; not so with graduate work in theology. In seminary I found that the workload was much more than I could handle in six days. I needed the seventh day for class preparation. Many of my classmates spent a significant portion of the day in study. However, my convictions would not be eroded by my circumstances. Even though there were many times when I could have benefited from using the day for study, I was glad to suffer the consequences as a means of honoring my Lord and doing His will.

My desire and ability to do what the Lord asks is not of my own effort. It is God who not only has called us to honor Him

but also has sent His only Son to die and to conquer the grave
for us. Those who surrender to Christ will find that they can
only live their lives through Him. He saves us and sanctifies
us. Christ alone enables us both to understand our call to work
and protects us from being dominated by it: We are not to be
ruled by creation. We are to enjoy the call to rest from our week
as we spend time worshipping Him.

In response to the criticisms of the Pharisees, Jesus said,
"The Sabbath was made for man, not man for the Sabbath. So
the Son of Man is Lord even of the Sabbath." (Mark 2:27-28)
Indeed, our Savior is Lord of the day of rest, a day that has been
given to us by Him for our benefit and blessing. It is truly a day
to exalt and praise Him.

── REFLECTION ──

Before reading this chapter, what have you thought
about maintaining a day of rest each week?

────

Do you believe that God is calling you to a day each
week where you honor Him by pausing from work and
worshipping Him? Please explain.

────

What challenges confront you in honoring
the Lord's Day?

────

What impact do you think the day of rest has upon
your life and that of others?

WORK EXCELLENCE

*L*ORD, I thank You for calling me both to work and to a weekly day of rest and worship. Please protect me from allowing the creation to dominate and control my life. For Your glory show me how to honor You with my rest and worship.

Chapter 10

God's Presence

P ETE had little difficulty deciding his career upon finishing high school: He entered the plumbing trade. First he
was an apprentice, then a journeyman, and finally a master
plumber. After working for one of the larger Baltimore shops in
the early 1950's, he entered into a partnership with his friend
Charlie. For decades their mechanical contracting company
provided excellent service for its many customers.

In time Pete moved away from the plumbing business and
worked as a developer, building homes. At his stage in life, selling his assets to make a bold career change could have been
foolish and possibly financially fatal. Building homes was
demanding. At times it appeared as though his new venture
might not succeed at all, because of government regulations
and other complications. However, buying large tracts of land
and building roads and houses proved to be a natural fit for

Pete's ability. His success in the former plumbing business paled in comparison to his work as a developer and builder. He provided well for his family. His fruitful labor enabled him to purchase homes and cars that satisfied his desires. He became a picture of success, the American dream. What he had set out to do was accomplished: His efforts were rewarded.

Pete is my father. What caused his success? The secular world would answer by pointing to his wise decisions, skill, back-breaking work, and persistence. Many would say that there was an element of luck. But was there an unseen cause of success? Is it possible that something else exists by which one benefits, but rarely acknowledges? I believe there is an unrecognized influence that my father understood and acknowledged. The Scriptures speak about just such a cause in the words penned by the great and glorious King Solomon:

> *A song of ascents. Of Solomon. Unless the LORD builds the house, its builders labor in vain. Unless the LORD watches over the city, the watchmen stand guard in vain.*
>
> *In vain you rise early and stay up late, toiling for food to eat—for he grants sleep to those he loves.*
>
> (PSALM 127:1-2)

King Solomon knew first-hand the reality of these words. He had inherited from his father the plans, resources and commission to build a temple to the one true God. The temple would be a glorious structure by all standards. I Kings 6 describes in detail the holy structure built with cut stone, its interior overlaid with cedar and gold. It took seven years to construct. Solomon and his subjects marked its completion with a celebration of worship to dedicate it to the Lord:

> *Then the king and all Israel with him offered sacrifices before the LORD. Solomon offered a sacrifice of fellowship offerings to the LORD: twenty-two thousand cattle and a hundred and twenty thousand sheep and goats.*
>
> (I KINGS 8: 62,63A)

The sacrifices and worship acknowledged that the seen world was not the total sum of all that existed. Solomon makes this very point in Psalm 127. This passage has many implications for all who engage in any form of work. Without an understanding of these truths, our thinking about work is distorted. Two aspects of this divine cause are mentioned here: God's presence and God's preservation.

GOD'S PRESENCE IN WORK

> *Unless the LORD builds the house, its builders labor in vain.*
>
> (V. I)

My wife Debby loves to be creative with her home. Painting, wallpapering, sewing drapes, and arranging flowers and furniture are some of her tools for designing a home. She has spent weeks needlepointing or smocking a dress. When Spring comes her attention is drawn to the outdoors: preparing and maintaining flowerbeds are among her favorite creative activities. Are these accomplishments to be attributed to Debby alone? Did God have a part to play in any of this? Solomon's words inform us that all Debby's accomplishments over the years have resulted from the presence of God. He gave her such desires, abilities, resources, and successes. Solomon reveals his world and life view in Psalm 127: nothing is built unless the Lord is present. It is by the will and providence of God that work is accomplished. The implications of this are significant.

Perhaps even for the Christian the response is, "But I have done all the work." What evidence is there that God was even partly involved, much less totally responsible? Genesis reminds us that God created us. Our whole being is from Him: This includes our ability to think creatively, carry out a process, and bring a plan to completion. The desires, abilities, and resources are all borrowed from God. God is the only one who has made something out of nothing. The desire to create and build, seen throughout all nations, comes not simply by process or evolution, but from the purposes of God. It is a part of our God-given nature.

In the Old Testament book of I Kings, chapter 5, King Solomon tells Hiram, king of Tyre, that his father David wanted to build the temple, but was not qualified. Why? Because many of the bordering nations were in adversarial relationships with Israel. Armed conflict characterized his kingship. The nation lacked peace. David had the plans and the resources, but not the presence and blessing of the Lord. God made it clear to David that it would be his son, Solomon, who would build the temple (2 Samuel 7).

What would have happened if David had attempted to build the temple in opposition to God's expressed will? In some ways it is hard to know. Perhaps it would have been completed. David remembered well, however, what had happened when the Ark of the Covenant had been brought in to Jerusalem in a manner inconsistent with God's Law. They had placed it on a new, ox-driven cart, guided by Uzzah. When the ox stumbled, Uzzah extended his hand to steady the ark. As a result, the Lord struck him dead. Why? His seemingly kind action was offensive to God. The ark was being improperly carried. (2 Samuel 6). David was angry at the display of God's anger. Yet, in time, the ark was properly brought into Jerusalem. God blessed the effort and all was well in the kingdom.

What shall we conclude? When things go badly with our work is this a sign that God is not present, that the efforts are not of the Lord and will be in vain? Abraham had been called by God to leave his home and go to the land of Canaan, yet he was unable to stay because of the famine. Jacob's son Joseph met many difficulties in his life and work, yet he was clearly in the Lord's will. How easy was it for Moses to ask Pharaoh to let the Israelites go? Pharaoh had made life more difficult for many of the Jews, even though God had been present. Did Nehemiah face opposition in rebuilding the wall of Jerusalem? The apostle Paul was confronted over and over again with difficulties in his ministry of building churches. And most significant to those who mistakenly believe that God's presence always dictates "heaven on earth" is the suffering of Christ. In his first sermon, Peter made this statement about Christ's work:

> *This man was handed over to you by God's set purpose and foreknowledge; and you, with the help of wicked men, put him to death by nailing him to the cross.*
>
> (ACTS 2:23)

There may be times when we will not know if the Lord is present in our work. There may be many occasions when we struggle and find work difficult. Unless we know that the work activity is offensive to God, we have every right to believe the Lord will be present and that our efforts are not in vain. It is our privilege to look to Him in faith when at work.

GOD'S PRESERVATION IN WORK

This passage mentions God's protection and preservation, another important dimension of work:

> *Unless the LORD watches over the city, the watchmen stand guard in vain.*
>
> (PSALM 127:2)

We exert much effort to protect what has been built or made. We pay for insurance policies, private guards, and municipal police. We treat our homes for termites or apply paint to ensure their longevity. We do whatever we can to protect our assets.

Yet if the Lord does not guard and protect, there is nothing anyone can do to prevent destruction.

King Zedekiah of Judah was twenty-one years old when he began his eleven-year reign in Jerusalem. He was known for being evil. The priests and people were increasingly unfaithful to God as well. They were stiff-necked and hard-hearted. In time, they defiled the temple of God. Yet the Lord was persistent in pursuing His people so that they might see their sin and repent. In response, they mocked God's messenger, Jeremiah, and ignored His word. They rejected God's protection, and in exchange received God's anger. We read in 2 Chronicles of the horrific consequences:

He (God) brought up against them the king of the Babylonians, who killed their young men with the sword in the sanctuary, and spared neither young man nor young woman, old man or aged. God handed all of them over to Nebuchadnezzar. He carried to Babylon all the articles from the temple of God, both large and small, and the treasures of the Lord's temple and the treasures of the king and his officials. They set fire to God's temple and broke down the wall of Jerusalem; they burned all the palaces and destroyed everything of value there.

He carried into exile to Babylon the remnant, who escaped from the sword, and they became servants to him and his sons until the kingdom of Persia came to power. The land enjoyed its Sabbath

rests; all the time of its desolation it rested, until
the seventy years were completed in fulfillment of
the word of the LORD spoken by Jeremiah

(2 CHRONICLES 36:17-21).

What had been a means of bringing glory to God was destroyed by Him. God would no longer have His city, temple or name defiled. It was far better to see it destroyed. All the guards and soldiers under Zedekiah could not protect the city that had fallen under the anger of God: The Lord would no longer be a part of its protection. God handed over the city to Nebuchadnezzar.

Does God provide and take away His protection today? The answer is yes. All that remains are the consequences of His protective presence. God uses people as His means of protection, but our efforts alone are not sufficient. When God withdraws His protective hand there will be consequences. There is nothing you can do. As Solomon says:

"In vain you rise early and stay up late, toiling for
food to eat—for he grants sleep to those he loves"

(PSALM. 127:2).

This does not mean that all destruction is the result of His anger as seen in the day of Zedekiah. We may not know why God withdraws His protection, only the consequences. We do know that God does all things for a purpose and design. As the apostle Paul says in his letter to the Christians in Rome:

And we know that in all things God works for the
good of those who love him, who have been called
according to his purpose.

(ROMANS 8:28)

CHRISTIAN AND NON-CHRISTIAN?

When considering Solomon's psalm, are we to make a distinction between the non-Christian and Christian? Is God
involved in the building project overseen by the atheist developer? Does he protect it during and after its completion? What
about all the nations of the world? Are we to believe that God
is somehow concerned and involved in blessing their efforts?

The answer is yes. People may erect walls separating the
spiritual and the secular. There may be no acknowledgment of
God. But there is never a time when God withdraws His presence. Solomon's father David says in Psalm 139, "Where can I
go from your Spirit? Where can I flee from your presence?"
(v.7) The answer is "Nowhere." The God who is present is
always active. He is not somehow too busy to care and give
oversight to his creation. He is as involved in the child's building a Tinkertoy house as He is in the construction of the
Empire State Building in New York City.

What I find amazing is that He is so benevolent. His goodness is experienced by all, no matter their belief or standing.
He causes His sun to rise on the evil and the good, and sends
rain on the righteous and the unrighteous (Matthew 5:45).
This reminder of God's common grace informs us that all

those who live on this earth receive the benefits of God's presence. All people of the world enjoy productive work. They live in communities and cities. With some exceptions they return to their apartments or homes and enjoy food. The Christians and non-Christians who inhabit the world and engage in the vast array of work experience the blessed presence of the Lord.

The world's plumbers and doctors have successful days whether they are Christian or not. The same is true for the farmer, teacher, stay-at-home mother, or nuclear scientist. None have the ability to accomplish anything without the grace of God. And nothing accomplished by them will last a moment longer than what God has decreed.

The one proper response to this truth is worship. Worship is always the test of work excellence. Acknowledging His active and gracious presence in this part of our lives takes our prideful eyes away from ourselves and focuses them on the One who is responsible for all accomplishments. May He always receive the glory and praise!

—— REFLECTION ——

How do you view success and disappointment when it comes to work?

———

What is your response when your efforts do not bring about the desired results?

———

Does it ever bother you that those who have no interest in God have such incredible success? How have you explained such achievement?

———

Do you ever struggle with responding in worship to what is taught in this passage?

———

Can you name examples of how the Lord will use this passage in your life and work?

WORK EXCELLENCE

*L*ORD, help me to discern your presence in all I do, especially within my work. Your Word informs me that nothing is accomplished as a result of my talents and efforts. You are the one who builds and preserves; yet, I am called to work and be productive. Help me understand these truths. Help me not to become vain and prideful in my accomplishments, but mindful of Your presence in my work.

Chapter 11

Daniel

Y OU are not alone. The New Testament book of Hebrews reminds us that a great cloud of witnesses in heaven, by the demonstration of their faith, influences us today. These people trusted God through difficult circumstances. The book of Hebrews tells us that they did not receive what had been promised. Daniel, in the Old Testament, stands as an example of what it means to take one's faith into a secular environment for the glory of God.

Daniel lived during the period of Israel's history known as the Exile. After the death of King Solomon the kingdom split. The northern portion of the kingdom eventually was taken over and dissipated by the Assyrians. Some years later, the southern kingdom met the destructive power of king Nebuchadnezzar, who transported many of the survivors to his home in Babylon. The rebellious Jewish people had experienced the wrath of God. It was in this context that the book of Daniel was penned. Some of the details of his life are given in the following passage:

In the third year of the reign of Jehoiakim king of Judah, Nebuchadnezzar king of Babylon came to Jerusalem and besieged it. And the Lord delivered Jehoiakim king of Judah into his hand, along with some of the articles from the temple of God. These he carried off to the temple of his god in Babylonia and put in the treasure house of his god.

Then the king ordered Ashpenaz, chief of his court officials, to bring in some of the Israelites from the royal family and the nobility— young men without any physical defect, handsome, showing aptitude for every kind of learning, well informed, quick to understand, and qualified to serve in the king's palace. He was to teach them the language and literature of the Babylonians The king assigned them a daily amount of food and wine from the king's table. They were to be trained for three years, and after that they were to enter the king's service. Among these were some from Judah: Daniel, Hananiah, Mishael and Azariah. The chief official gave them new names: to Daniel, the name Belteshazzar; to Hananiah, Shadrach; to Mishael, Meshach; and to Azariah, Abednego.

> *But Daniel resolved not to defile himself with*
> *the royal food and wine, and he asked the chief offi-*
> *cial for permission not to defile himself this way.*

(DANIEL 1 : 1 -8)

Daniel and his friends found themselves employed by a powerful boss in a distant and strange city. Before looking at the nature of Daniel's work and experience, consider the temperament of his employer/king, Nebuchadnezzar.

THE KING BOSS

In approximately 600 BC, Judah fell under the power of King Nebuchadnezzar. Some years later he declared the king of Judah, Zedekiah, to be in rebellion. What were the consequences? He besieged Jerusalem until the people were starving to death. The Babylonian army broke down the walls and gates and destroyed houses and important buildings. Zedekiah and his army, afraid for their lives, ran for the plains of Jericho. Their attempt to escape was futile. They were overtaken and captured. When the rebellious king was taken before Nebuchadnezzar, the Babylonian king ordered each of Zedekiah's sons slaughtered before his sight. Then they put out Zedekiah's eyes, placed his feet in shackles, and led him off to Babylon.

Years later King Nebuchadnezzar gave orders to make an image of gold. Everyone in the kingdom was to bow and worship the image upon hearing the sound of the musical instruments. It was reported that three Jewish men refused to obey the king's decree. This news outraged the powerful monarch who ordered the three to be thrown into a blazing furnace. The sentence was carried out, and they were cast into a fire that should have instantly killed them. But the men miraculously survived by the hand of a much greater king, the God of the universe.

These are only two of many occasions of this king's anger. He was not a boss you would ever cross or disappoint. What would have happened if you had overslept and arrived late for work in the palace? It would happen only once; there would be no second chance.

What would it be like to display your faith in the Lord when working under such circumstances? It would certainly be tempting to conceal your faith as a means of preserving your life. But this was not an option for Daniel.

FAITH TESTED

Daniel served as a statesman at the court of this heathen king. There was little in common between the kingdom of Daniel's Lord and that of Nebuchadnezzar.

Daniel and his exiled friends were chosen for their exceptional abilities. These young and attractive men represented Israel's royal families and nobility. They had to be bright and intelligent, capable of learning the language and literature of this strange kingdom. For three years they were trained by the chief court official, Ashpenza, before being presented to the king.

During this period of training, Daniel and his friends ate from the king's table. This tested Daniel's faith because some of the food served was used in the worship of idols. According to verse 8, Daniel resolved not to defile himself with the food and wine.

If I request a change in work schedule or responsibilities, I may lose my coming promotion or salary increase. I could even find myself looking for another job if my request irritates my employer. But for Daniel to decide not to defile himself and to request a different food and wine menu was synonymous with losing his head.

For three years Daniel trained for the royal service. It must have been a constant challenge for him to learn a secular system in a foreign land. He must have longed for his home in Judah. In Babylon he missed the familiar sacrifices and offerings, the worship at the temple built by Solomon. The annual Jewish feast would not have been observed. He had no hope that life would return to previously familiar ways. Such a change would cause bitterness and resentment in most of us, and would make life difficult for others. Yet this is where we see Daniel's faith working itself out.

Daniel accepted his circumstances and worked diligently. He was not consumed with his loss. Instead, his life won the respect of those over him. His position was influential even though he had no seniority. This Jewish man was not going to ignore the truth of Scriptures.

The Law specifically discloses God's will. He commands against idolatry (Exodus 20). To eat food used in some form of idol worship would have indicated that Daniel agreed with the practice. However, he did not take a position of superiority. He was gracious in dealing with his supervisor, Ashpenaz. He humbly made his request, knowing that it challenged common sense. If Ashpenaz were to change those things that Nebuchadnezzer had ordered, such as the wine and food, then he could be charged and beheaded. Daniel, knowing this all too well, requested that Ashpenaz consider and possibly accept the following appeal:

"Please test your servants for ten days: Give us nothing but vegetables to eat and water to drink. Then compare our appearance with that of the young men who eat the royal food, and treat your servants in accordance with what you see." So he agreed to this and tested them for ten days.

(DANIEL 1 : 12-14)

This picture of faith appeals to one's senses. Ashpenaz knew nothing of this Hebrew's faith. Daniel demonstrated an unusual ability in ministering to this secular culture by presenting his request. At the end of the ten-day test, Daniel and his friends looked considerably better than those who had eaten the king's food and wine. The king's foods were removed and vegetables became the regular diet for Daniel and his friends. At the end of the three years Ashpenaz presented them before the king to be examined. The results? They were far superior to all the others.

Applying our faith in the work culture is more than a challenge; it is our calling as believers. Even 2,600 years later, Daniel remains a dynamic illustration of this. He applied truth in a context of grace and sensitivity to those around him. Did anyone come to faith through this exchange? We do not know all that took place and how the Lord used it then. Daniel certainly influenced his Jewish friends. In time Daniel's witness in the secular workplace impacted Nebuchadnezzar. By the end of Daniel 4, Nebuchadnezzar is seen worshiping God:

> *Then I praised the Most High; I honored and glorified him who lives forever. His dominion is an eternal dominion; his kingdom endures from generation to generation. All the peoples of the earth are regarded as nothing. He does as he pleases with the powers of heaven and the peoples of the earth. No one can hold back his hand or say to him: "What have you done?" At the same time that my sanity was restored, my honor and splendor were returned to me for the glory of my kingdom. My advisers and nobles sought me out, and I was restored to my throne and became even greater than before. Now I, Nebuchadnezzar, praise and exalt and glorify the King of heaven, because everything he does is right and all his ways are just. And those who walk in pride he is able to humble.*
>
> (DANIEL 4:34B-37)

Perhaps your position will not allow you to influence kings and those who serve them. But you do have influence, whether great or small. Your understanding and practice of the ways of God in work will impact your own life and others in your generation. God wants the gospel to be present in us. God's grace, through Christ, will cause a witness such as Daniel's to be evident in our lives. There is no true excellence in work if the gospel is absent. The gospel not only brings us to a saving relationship with the Lord, but also transforms our lives, including our work and careers.

May our Lord be gracious to you and those with whom you work. May He transform their lives for His glory.

——— REFLECTION ———

How often do you pray for those with
and for whom you work?
What is the content of your prayers?

———

Have you ever been in a situation at work
in which you were asked to
compromise your commitment to Christ?
How did you respond?

———

What changes might occur if you
lived your faith in the workplace?
Is it only a matter of telling others about
Christ and His finished work on the cross?

———

In what ways do you believe that God will use you in
the lives of others with whom you work?

WORK EXCELLENCE

LORD of Heaven, the world and its work places do not recognize You or Your Word. Please use me in my place of work to be the "salt and light" like Daniel. By Your grace help me to know what to say that will draw others to You. May my friends be drawn to You and Your love, for the glory of our Savior, Jesus Christ.